The Write Word at the Right Time
By
Lawrence W. Gold

The Write Word at the Right Time © 2020 by Lawrence W. Gold

All rights reserved. No part of this book may be reproduced or transmitted in any form or by any means, electronic or mechanical, including photocopying, recording or by any information storage and retrieval system, without permission in writing from the publisher.

A Grass Valley Publishing Production

ISBN 978-1-736-3960-1-8

Cover Art © 2020 by Theresa McCracken

Book design by Aaxel Author Services & Noah Adam Paperman

TABLE OF CONTENTS

Section 1: Introduction   **1**

Section 2: The Charts   **5**

Section 3: Useful Advice   **57**

SECTION I

INTRODUCTION

I've been writing novels for over ten years. Like most new novelists, I read everything in sight and learned much. Even as I gradually developed my craft, problems would arise during the writing process. I'd rush to the Internet to OneLook Thesaurus (https://www.onelook.com) and MasterWriter (https://app.masterwriter.com). Both were useful in unique ways and to this date I continue to use them.

Despite the growth of television, movies, and online entertainment, creative writing, though tattered, persists. Moreover, creative writing has grown from the print page, to the electronic page, and finally to the audiobook. The predicted demise of reading, to paraphrase Mark Twain: has been greatly exaggerated.

Writers, being creatures of habit, find themselves using words repeatedly.

Sooner or later, we notice the multitude of saids, smiles, walks, laughs and other descriptive terms. We reach first for the thesaurus, for adjectives and God forbid, for the adverb to modify the descriptions, and finally, working hard, we search for unique means of making the descriptions more meaningful and more accurate. As nature hates a void, the search for better descriptions has spawned hundreds of books and websites dedicated to finding the right word. Many are excellent, comprehensive, well-researched, and wise in their topic selections. If any fault exists, it's that they're too complete, too exhaustive, and too difficult to use (812 synonyms for walked had me nodding off). Hence, this little book: *The Write Word at the Right Time*.

We all seek original thought, but how many of us can do that on cue? Oscar Wilde in the 19th century said, "Good writers borrow, great writers steal."

The business metaphor of, Reinventing the Wheel, is as potent and appropriate today as it was in the 1970s when it was first introduced.

With the mantra of not reinventing the wheel, my writing has, over time, lead me to search for improved ways to write common words and phrases. Long searches eventually lead to smaller lists, while incomplete, were spot on for the words I sought. No longer did they leave me with bellowing, or giggling, or simpering but offered me words more appropriate to my style and ways of expression.

The Write Word at the Right Time is a compilation of abbreviated lists and ideas that sit at my left hand as I write. In addition, I've included advice that's been useful to me. For the most part, the tables are more succinct and thus more useful than other compilations I've seen. I hope they are as useful to you as they have been for me. Longer tables crept in because to abbreviate them required a vacuum rather than a delete key, hence a few remain.

Apologies to my professors of English, Creative Writing, and talented editors for my errors of omission and commission. As a physician, I wrote to make my thoughts clear although my handwriting was, too often, nearly unreadable (thank God for nurses who could decipher).

Lawrence W. Gold

SECTION II

THE CHARTS

SUBSTITUTES FOR 'BECAUSE'

Don't automatically replace "because." It may be the perfect word.

As	In light
As a consequence	In that
As a result	In view of the fact that
As long as	Inasmuch as
As things go	Knowing as how
Being that	Now what
By reason	On account
By virtue	On the grounds that
Consequently	Out
Considering	Owing to
Due to	Seeing that
For	Since
For reason that	Thanks to
For the sake	Therefore
Forasmuch as	Though
Given that	

SUBSTITUTES FOR 'FEEL'

Accept	Have a hunch	Resign oneself to
Allow	I believe	Sense
Appreciate	I guess	Spot
Aware	I hear you	Stomach
Be conscious	Intuit	Submit to
Comprehend	I suppose	Succumb to
Conclude	I think	Suffer
Deal with	Know	Surrender to
Descry	Live through	Survive
Determine	Live with	Tolerate
Discern	Notice	Undergo
Endure	Observe	Weather
Enjoy	Perceive	Withstand
Experience	Put up with	Yield to
Face	Reconcile oneself to	
Grasp	Remain	

SUBSTITUTES FOR 'LAUGH'

Belly-laugh	Giggle	Snicker
Break up	Guffaw	Snigger
Cachinnate	Hee-haw	Split (one's) sides
Cackle	Horselaugh	Titter
Chortle	Howl	Twitter
Chuckle	Jeer	Whooped
Crack up	Roared	Yowled
Crow	Scoff	

SUBSTITUTES FOR 'SAID'

Don't fear the use of "said," as alternatives can be worse.

Accused	Corrected	Mumbled	Sighed
Added	Cried	Murmured	Simpered
Affirmed	Declared	Muttered	Snapped
Agreed	Demanded	Objected	Snarled
Answered	Disagreed	Ordered	Sneered
Argued	Exclaimed	Pleaded	Sobbed
Asked	Explained	Proclaimed	Spat
Asserted	Gasped	Promised	Squeaked
Barked	Giggled	Protested	Squealed
Bellowed	Groaned	Purred	Stated
Blurted	Growled	Replied	Tittered
Breathed	Grumbled	Roared	Vowed
Cautioned	Gurgled	Scolded	Wailed
Chuckled	Implored	Screamed	Warbled
Complained	Insisted	Shouted	Whispered
Confirmed	Laughed	Shrieked	Yelled

SUBSTITUTES FOR 'SEXY'

Alluring	Fetching	Seductive
Arousing	First-rate	Sensual
Awesome	Flirtatious	Spicy
Beguiling	Foxy	Steamy
Bewitching	Hot	Stunning
Captivating	Irresistible	Sultry
Coquettish	Luscious	Tantalizing
Delectable	Mesmerizing	Tasty
Desirable	Nubile	Tempting
Enticing	Provocative	Voluptuous
Entrancing	Radiant	Winsome
Erotic	Saucy	

"STATE OF BEING" WORDS

PASSIVE

Am	Could	Have	Should
Are	Did	Is	Was
Be	Do	May	Were
Been	Does	Might	Will
Being	Had	Must	Would
Can	Has	Shall	

The man **was** walking on the platform.

                vs.

                The man strode along the platform.

Jim **is** a lover of country living.

                vs.

                Jim treasures country living.

There **are** three things that make me feel the way I do.

                vs.

                Three things convince me.

INSTEAD OF SUDDENLY, USE:

Abruptly

All at once

All of a sudden

At once

At that moment

Forthwith

From nowhere

Immediately

In a flash

In an instant

Instantly

Just then

Out of the blue

Promptly

Straightaway

Swiftly

Unexpectedly

With precipitous speed

Without delay

Without hesitation

Without notice

Without warning

A "VERY" SPECIAL PROBLEM

Avoid using the word "very" because it's lazy.
A man isn't tired, he's exhausted.
"Don't use very sad, use morose." - N.H. Kleinbaum

Afraid	**Terrified**
Angry	**Furious**
Bad	**Atrocious**
Beautiful	**Exquisite**
Big	**Immense**
Bright	**Dazzling**
Capable	**Accomplished**
Clean	**Spotless**
Clever	**Brilliant**
Cold	**Freezing**
Conventional	**Conservative**
Dirty	**Squalid**
Dry	**Parched**
Eager	**Keen**
Fast	**Quick**
Fierce	**Ferocious**
Good	**Superb**
Happy	**Jubilant**

THE CHARTS

Hot	**Scalding**
Hungry	**Ravenous**
Large	**Colossal**
Lively	**Vivacious**
Loved	**Adored**
Neat	**Immaculate**
Old	**Ancient**
Poor	**Destitute**
Pretty	**Beautiful**
Quiet	**Silent**
Risky	**Perilous**
Roomy	**Spacious**
Rude	**Vulgar**
Serious	**Solemn**
Small	**Tiny**
Strong	**Unyielding**
Stupid	**Idiotic**

CONTINUED ▼

A "VERY" SPECIAL PROBLEM (CONT'D)

Tasty	**Delicious**
Thin	**Gaunt**
Tired	**Exhausted**
Ugly	**Hideous**
Valuable	**Precious**
Weak	**Feeble**
Wet	**Soaked**
Wicked	**Villainous**
Wise	**Sagacious**
Worried	**Anxious**

ALTERNATIVES TO 'WALK'

Amble	Limp	Promenade	Stalk
Bounce	Lumber	Prowl	Step
Caper	Lurch	Pussyfoot	Stomp
Careen	March	Ramble	Stride
Cavort	Meander	Roam	Stroll
Clump	Mince	Rove	Strut
Clump	Mosey	Sashay	Stumble
Falter	Pace	Saunter	Stump
Flounder	Pad	Scuff	Tiptoe
Foot it	Parade	Scurry	Toddle
Footslog	Perambulate	Shamble	Traipse
Gimp	Peregrinate	Shuffle	Tramp
Hike	Plod	Skulk	Trudge
Hobble	Pound	Slink	Waddle
Hoof it	Power walk	Somnambulate	
Leg it	Prance	Stagger	

ALTERNATIVES TO 'WENT'

Ambled	Fled	Paraded	Sprinted
Approached	Flew	Pounced	Stomped
Ascended	Full	Pushed On	Stormed Out
Barreled	Galloped	Raced	Strode
Bolted	Glided	Ran	Strutted
Burst	Hiked	Retreated	Traipsed
Climbed	Hurried	Roamed	Traveled
Crawled	Hurtled	Rolled	Trekked
Crept	Hustled	Rushed	Tripped
Darted	Jogged	Sauntered	Tumbled
Dashed	Jumped	Skated	Vanished
Dove	Left	Slid	Veered
Escaped	Marched	Slithered	Waddled
Exited	Meandered	Soared	Walked
Faded	Neared	Sped	Zoomed

THE CHARTS

BODY TYPES

Agile	Colossal	Fit
Ample	Compact	Flabby
Angular	Corpulent	Flat-Chested
Anorexic	Curvy	Fleshy
Awkward	Dainty	Flexible
Barrel Chested	Defined	Frail
Big	Delicate	Full
Big-Bellied	Developed	Full-Grown
Bodily	Dimpled	Gangly
Bony	Distended	Gargantuan
Brawny	Drooping	Generous
Brisk	Dumpy	Giant
Broad	Dwarfish	Gigantic
Bulbous	Elephantine	Goliath
Bulging	Elfin	Graceful
Busty	Elongated	Growing
Buxom	Emaciated	Heavy
Calloused	Fast	Herculean
Chubby	Fat	Huge
Chunky	Firm	Hulking

CONTINUED ▽

BODY TYPES (CONT'D)

Humpbacked	Mammoth	Puny
Hunched	Massive	Quick
Hurried	Measly	Rotund
Husky	Mighty	Rounded
Immense	Muscular	Runty
Itsy-Bitsy	Narrow	Sawed-Off
Jumbo	Nimble	Scrawny
Lanky	Obese	Sculpted
Large	Overweight	Shrimpy
Lean	Paunchy	Shriveled
Leggy	Peg-Legged	Shrunken
Limber	Petite	Sinewy
Limp	Plodding	Sizable
Lithe	Plump	Skeletal
Little	Podgy	Skinny
Loitering	Ponderous	Slender
Long-Legged	Portly	Slim
Long-Limbed	Potbellied	Slinky
Lumbering	Protruding	Slouched
Lumpy	Pudgy	Slow

Sluggish	Streamlined	Top-Heavy
Small	Stubby	Towering
Small-Waisted	Stumpy	Tremendous
Soft	Stunted	Trim
Solid	Substantial	Tubby
Spindly	Supple	Underfed
Spiny	Svelte	Undersized
Spry	Sweating	Underweight
Square	Swift	Unhurried
Squat	Swift-Moving	Voluptuous
Stacked	Tall	Wee
Starved	Teeny	Wide
Stiff	Thick	Willowy
Stocky	Thickset	Wiry
Stout	Thin	Withered
Strapping	Toned	Wobbly

COLOR AND VISUAL QUALITIES

Amber	Chocolate	Fuchsia	Magenta
Amethyst	Chrome	Garnet	Mahogany
Aqua	Citrine	Gay	Maize
Aquamarine	Claret	Glassy	Maroon
Avocado	Clear	Gold	Mauve
Azure	Cobalt	Green	Milky
Black	Copper	Grizzly	Milky
Blue	Coral	Henna	Mint
Brass	Cordovan	Indigo	Mustard
Bright	Cream	Iridescent	Navy
Brilliant	Crimson	Ivory	Obsidian
Brindle	Crystalline	Jade	Ocher
Bronze	Cyan	Jet	Olive
Buff	Dark	Khaki	Onyx
Burgundy	Drab	Lake	Opaque
Carmine	Dull	Lavender	Orange
Cerise	Dun	Lemon	Orchid
Charcoal	Emerald	Light	Pale
Chartreuse	Flesh	Lilac	Peach
Chestnut	Flushed	Lime	Pearl

THE CHARTS

Pearly	Rose	Shimmering	Transparent
Pearly	Ruby	Sienna	Turquoise
Pink	Ruddy	Silver	Ultramarine
Plum	Rust	Slate	Umber
Plum	Sable	Smoky	Vermillion
Poppy	Saffron	Snowy	Violet
Primrose	Salmon	Sooty	Walnut
Puce	Sapphire	Tan	White
Purple	Scarlet	Topaz	Wine
Red	Sepia	Translucent	Yellow

DESCRIBING EYE COLOR

Amber	Crystal Blue	Mahogany
Aquamarine	Denim Blue	Mink Brown
Ash Gray	Electric Blue	Mocha
Azure Lake Blue	Emerald	Moss Green
Cerulean	Glacial Blue	Pewter Smoky
Chestnut	Gray	Platinum
Chocolate Brown	Gray Dove	Sapphire
Chrome	Gray Fog	Sepia
Cocoa Brown	Gray Olive	Sienna Brown
Coffee Brown	Gray Shark	Storm Blue Slate
Cognac	Gray Silver	Turquoise
Concrete	Gunmetal	
Copper	Leaf Green	

WORDS TO DESCRIBE FACES

Angry	Dirty	Grim
Anxious	Dour	Grotesque
Bearded	Eager	Haggard
Beautiful	Enigma	Handsome
Black	Expectant	Happy
Blank	Expressionless	Hideous
Brick	Fair	Human
Bright	False	Ice
Broad	Familiar	Impassive
Brown	Famous	Inner
Calm	Fierce	Innocent
Cement	Flat	Jovial
Cheerful	Flushed	Lovely
Chiseled	Fresh	Opposite
Clean	Friendly	Outer
Corrugated	Frightened	Pale
Crystal	Funny	Pallid
Curious	Furrowed	Parallel
Dark	Gaunt	Pinched
Dead	Grave	Pleasant

CONTINUED

WORDS TO DESCRIBE FACES (CONT'D)

Pretty	Strange	Unlined
Red	Sullen	Upturned
Round	Sweet	Vertical
Sad	Thin	Weather-Beaten
Serious	Tired	White
Smooth	Triangular	Wrinkled
Solemn	Ugly	Wry
Stern	Unfamiliar	Yellow

LIPS DESCRIBED

Ashen	Eager	Mortal	Slack
Bearded	Eloquent	Narrow	Soft
Beautiful	Fat	Open	Stiff
Black	Feverish	Pale	Straight
Bloodless	Fleshy	Pallid	Suddenly
Bloody	Fresh	Perfect	Sweet
Blue	Full	Pink	Swollen
Cherry	Generous	Plump	Thick
Childish	Gray	Proud	Thin
Cold	Grim	Purple	Thirsty
Colorless	Hard	Red	Tight
Coral	Hot	Ripe	Top Heavy
Crimson	Human	Rosy	Tremulous
Cruel	Innocent	Ruddy	Warm
Curved	Livid	Scarlet	Wet
Dark	Long	Sensitive	White
Dead	Loose	Sensual	Wide
Dear	Loving	Sensuous	Withered
Delicate	Mobile	Short	Wrinkled
Dry	Moist	Silent	

NOSES DESCRIBED

All-encompassing	Charming	Gross	Pointy
Alluring	Chic	Gruesome	Pretty
Ample	Chubby	Handsome	Prominent
Angular	Compact	Hatchet-like	Protuberant
Appealing	Dapper	Hideous	Repugnant
Aquiline	Debonair	Homely	Repulsive
Attractive	Diminutive	Hooked	Ruthless
Ballooned	Disgusting	Hooter	Squashed
Barbed	Distinctive	Huge	Straight
Beaky	Distinguished	Impertinent	Subtle
Bent	Eagle-like	Insignificant	Thick
Big	Elegant	Insolent	Trim
Blunt	Engaging	Interesting	Turned up
Bony	Enormous	Jagged	Ugly
Bounteous	Expansive	Little	Unattractive
Broad	Forthright	Mean	Unsightly
Bulbous	Glamorous	Miniature	Vague
Button	Graceful	Petite	Warped

SMELL SUGGESTIONS

Acid	Lime	Redolent
Acrid	Loamy	Rose
Biting	Minty	Rotten
Dirty	Moist	Scent
Doggy (Outdoor Doggy)	Moldy	Sharp
Earthy	Musty	Skunky
Fetid	Nauseating	Sour
Fishy (Mildewed)	Odor	Spicy
Flowery	Perfumed	Spoiled
Fragrance	Petrichor	Stinking
Fresh	Plastic	Sweaty
Lemon	Pungent	Sweet
Lilac	Putrid	Tart

TYPES OF SMILES

Beam	Forced	Sardonic
Brittle	Genuine	Set
Broad	Gratuitous	Sly
Broadly	Grin	Smug
Cheesy	Gummy	Taut
Closed-lip	Humorless	Thin
Dominant	Lazy	Tremulous
Embarrassed	Loving	Twisted
Fake	Mirthless	Victory
Fearful	Mona Lisa	Wistful
Flirtatious	Polite	

VERBS FOR SMILES

Achieve	Extract	Permit
Answer with	Fades	Plays
Bestow	Flash	Provoke
Conceal	Flashes	Reassures
Confronts	Flickers	Renders
Contorts	Grant	Repress
Creases	Hides	Reveals
Crinkle into	Illuminate with	Rouse
Crinkles	Induce	Share
Deludes	Lightens	Shed
Departs	Lingers	Suppress
Disconcerts	Loosen	Twitches
Disparages	Manage	Wear
Extinguish	Mock	Wrinkle into

SMILE ADJECTIVES

Abrupt	Beautiful	Complaisant	Deprecating
Affectionate	Beguiling	Complicated	Derisive
Agreeable	Benign	Conceited	Devilish
Airy	Big	Conciliatory	Diabolical
Ambrosial	Bitter	Condescending	Dim
Amiable	Bland	Contagious	Disarming
Angelic	Blossomed	Contemptuous	Disdainful
Angry	Boyish	Convenient	Doubtful
Antiseptic	Brave	Courageous	Dubious
Apologetic	Brilliant	Courteous	Eager Naked
Approving	Brittle	Covert	Enamored
Arch	Broad	Crafty	Endearing
Ardent	Buoyant	Crooked	Endless
Artificial	Calm	Curious	Engaging
Atoning	Cautious	Cynical	Envious
Audible	Charming	Dawning	Everlasting
Bashful	Cheerful.	Dazzling	Excited
Beaming	Childlike	Deadly	Facile
Beaming	Clear	Debonair	Faded
Beatific	Complacent	Delightful	Faint

THE CHARTS

Fake	Hideous	Ingratiating	Maternal
False	Hollow	Innocent	Meaning
Fascinating	Hospitable	Insipid	Meek
Fawning	Hot	Inviting	Mellow
Fitful	Humorous	Involuntary	Metallic
Flattering	Hungry	Ironical	Mischievous
Fleeting	Icy	Ironical	Mischievous
Forced	Idiotic	Irradiating	Mocking
Frank	Illumined	Irrepressible	Moonshine
Frigid	Immortal	Joyless	Moony
Gentle	Immutable	Joyous	Mournful
Ghastly	Impish	Kind	Murderous
Girlish	Imploring	Large	Mutual
Glowing	Incandescent	Listless	Nasty
Gracious	Incisive	Little	Naughty
Grave	Incredulous	Lovely	Nervous
Greasy	Indifferent	Loving	New Quiet
Grim	Indomitable	Lurid	Obnoxious
Haughty	Indulgent	Malevolent	Pale Ready
Haughty	Infectious	Malicious	Parting

CONTINUED ▽

SMILE ADJECTIVES (CONT'D)

Passing	Rapid	Satirical	Somber
Paternal	Rare	Saturnine	Sparkling
Patient	Rascally	Saucy	Special
Patronizing	Ravished	Scornful	Speculative
Peculiar	Reassuring	Seductive	Spicy
Perpetual	Regretful	Senile	Sudden
Pert	Religious	Severe	Superior
Phony	Reluctant	Sexy	Surprised
Pitying	Reminiscent	Shy	Sustaining
Placid	Responding	Sickly	Sweet
Playful	Restless	Sidelong	Sympathetic
Polished	Restrained	Simulated	Thoughtless
Polite	Ridiculous	Sinister	Timid
Practiced	Roguish	Sly	Timid
Priceless	Rueful	Smarmy	Timorous
Prodigal	Rustic	Smart	Tolerant
Provocative	Sad	Smothered	Tolerant
Quizzical	Sagacious	Sneering	Unctuous
Racked	Sarcastic	Social	Uneasy
Radiant	Sardonic	Solitary	Vague

THE CHARTS

Vapid	Warm	Whimsical	Wistful
Vivacious	Watery	Wide	Wondering
Waking	Weary	Wild	Wreathed
Wan	Welcoming	Winning	Wry

SOUNDS

Bank	Hushed	Screech
Bark	Husky	Shriek
Boom	Lapping	Shrill
Buzz	Loud	Sloshing
Coo	Melodious	Snapping
Crackling	Moan	Snarl
Crash	Muffled	Snort
Crunching	Mumble	Softly
Cry	Murmur	Splash
Deafening	Mutter	Squeak
Echoing	Noisy	Squeal
Faint	Pealing	Thud
Groan	Pop	Thumb
Growl	Purring	Thundering
Gurgling	Quietly	Tinkle
Harsh	Raspy	Wail
Haw	Reverberating	Whimper
Hiss	Rumble	Whine
Hoarse	Rustle	Whisper
Howl	Scream	Whistling

VOICES DESCRIBED

Adenoidal	Husky	Smoky
Booming	Low (deep)	Soft-spoken
Brittle	Low (weak)	Sotto voce
Croaky	Matter of fact	Stentorian
Dead	Modulated (controlled)	Strangled
Disembodied	Monotonous	Strident
Dulcet	Nasal	Taut
Flat	Penetrating	Throaty
Foghorn-like	Quavering	Toneless
Fruity	Quiet	Tremulous
Grating	Raucous	Wheezy
Gravelly	Rough	Wobbly
Hoarse	Shrill	
Honeyed	Singsong	

WORDS: BEAUTIFUL, FUN, AND UNUSUAL

Abyssopelagic: the deep regions of the ocean or the abyss.
Acquiesce: submit or comply silently.
Akimbo: hands are on your hips with your elbows out.
Ameliorate: to make or become better, more bearable, or more satisfactory.
Aurora: radiation emissions create a natural display of lights and colors in the sky.
Becoming: attractive.
Blossoming: state of flowering or to flourish and develop.
Comely: attractive.
Dalliance: a brief love affair.
Delicacy: tasty and often expensive food.
Denouement: the resolution of a mystery.
Diaphanous: sheer and light; almost transparent.
Elixir: a medicinal or alchemic concoction.
Epiphany: a sudden, profound realization or idea.
Felicity: happiness or bliss.
Furtive: shifty, sneaky.
Galactic: adjective referring to galaxies.
Gossamer: the finest piece of thread, a spider's silk.
Harbinger: messenger with news from the future.

Idyllic:	happy, peaceful, or picturesque.
Illicit:	not legally permitted.
Imbue:	to infuse, instill.
Incendiary:	something that incites agitation or sedition- Flammable.
Inure:	to become jaded.
Lagniappe ("lah-*nyapp.*"):	for a gift, usually monetary like a tip.
Languor:	means lack of energy or vitality.
Limerence:	intense feelings of obsession or infatuation with another person.
Loquacious:	a nicer-sounding way to say that someone is talkative or chatty.
Mellifluous:	sweetly or smoothly flowing.
Panacea:	something that can heal or cure anything or, more generally, solve any problem.
Petrichor:	the distinctive smell that the air and the ground take on after it rains.
Phosphenes:	moving illusions you see after you rub your eyes.
Plethora:	a very large amount of something, an abundance.
Pyrrhic:	successful with heavy losses.

CONTINUED ▼

WORDS: BEAUTIFUL, FUN, AND UNUSUAL (CONT'D)

Quadrivium: the intersection of four roads.
Quintessence: the purest, most perfect embodiment of something.
Redolent: fragrant.
Sanguinolency: something bloody or something related to blood.
Serendipity: good luck or happy accidents.
Serene: calm, peaceful, tranquil.
Sibilance: the distinctive hiss-like sound made by the letter S.
Silhouette: shadow with a more pleasant connotation.
Succulent: juicy.
Superfluous: unnecessary or excessive.
Syzygy: an alignment of celestial bodies or planets.
Taradiddle: a false statement or bit of nonsense.
Tranquility: the state of being calm or peaceful.
Vellichor: the appealing mystique of an old bookshop.

GREAT ADJECTIVES; USE JUDICIOUSLY

Adamant:	unyielding
Adroit:	clever, resourceful
Amatory:	sexual
Animistic:	reversion to earlier form
Antic:	clownish, frolicsome
Arcadian:	serene
Baleful:	deadly, foreboding
Bellicose:	quarrelsome
Bilious:	unpleasant, peevish
Boorish:	crude, insensitive
Calamitous:	disastrous
Caustic:	corrosive, sarcastic
Cerulean:	sky blue
Comely:	attractive
Concomitant:	accompanying
Contumacious:	rebellious
Corpulent:	obese
Crapulous:	immoderate appetite
Defamatory:	maliciously misrepresenting
Didactic:	conveying information or morality
Dilatory:	causing delay, tardy

CONTINUED

GREAT ADJECTIVES; USE JUDICIOUSLY (CONT'D)

Dowdy:	shabby, old-fashioned
Efficacious:	producing a desired effect
Effulgent:	brilliantly radiant
Egregious:	conspicuous, flagrant
Endemic:	prevalent, native
Equanimous:	even, balanced
Execrable:	wretched, detestable
Fastidious:	meticulous, overly delicate
Feckless:	weak, irresponsible
Fecund:	prolific, inventive
Friable:	brittle
Fulsome:	abundant, overdone, effusive
Garrulous:	wordy, talkative
Guileless:	naive
Gustatory:	having to do with taste or eating
Heuristic:	learning through trial-and-error
Histrionic:	affected, theatrical
Hubristic:	proud, excessively self-confident
Incendiary:	inflammatory, combustible, hot
Insidious:	subtle, seductive, treacherous
Insolent:	impudent, contemptuous

Intransigent:	uncompromising
Inveterate:	habitual, persistent
Invidious:	resentful, envious, obnoxious
Irksome:	annoying
Jejune:	dull, puerile
Jocular:	jesting, playful
Judicious:	discreet
Lachrymose:	tearful,
Limpid:	simple, transparent, serene
Loquacious:	talkative
Luminous:	clear, shining
Mannered:	artificial, stilted
Mendacious:	deceptive
Meretricious:	whorish, pretentious
Minatory:	menacing
Mordant:	biting, incisive, pungent
Munificent:	lavish, generous
Nefarious:	wicked
Noxious:	harmful, corrupting
Obtuse:	blunt, stupid
Parsimonious:	frugal, restrained

GREAT ADJECTIVES; USE JUDICIOUSLY (CONT'D)

Pendulous:	suspended, indecisive
Pernicious:	injurious, deadly
Pervasive:	widespread
Petulant:	rude, ill humored
Platitudinous:	dull or banal comments
Precipitate:	steep, speedy
Propitious:	auspicious, benevolent
Puckish:	impish
Querulous:	cranky, whining
Quiescent:	inactive, untroublesome
Rebarbative:	irritating, repellent
Recalcitrant:	resistant, obstinate
Redolent:	aromatic, evocative
Rhadamanthine:	harshly strict
Risible:	laughable
Ruminative:	contemplative
Sagacious:	wise, discerning
Salubrious:	healthful
Sartorial:	relating to attire, tailored
Sclerotic:	hardening
Serpentine:	snake-like, tempting or wily

Spasmodic:	having to do with a spasm
Strident:	harsh, obtrusively loud
Taciturn:	closemouthed, reticent
Tenacious:	persistent, cohesive
Tremulous:	nervous, trembling
Trenchant:	sharp, distinct
Turbulent:	restless, tempestuous
Turgid:	swollen, pompous
Ubiquitous:	pervasive, widespread
Uxorious:	too affectionate or compliant
Verdant:	green, unripe
Voluble:	glib, given to speaking
Voracious:	ravenous, insatiable
Wheedling:	flattering
Withering:	devastating
Zealous:	eager, devoted

USING SIMPLER WORDS

"Poor Faulkner. Does he really think big emotions come from big words?" - Ernest Hemingway

Acceded	Agreed
Accommodate	Serve
Accomplish	Do
Accumulate	Gather
Adaptability	Adapt
Affirmative	Yes
Aggregate	Total
Ameliorate	Improve
Ascertain	Learn
Cognizant	Aware
Compel	Force
Compensate	Pay
Component	Part
Concerning	About
Demonstrate	Show
Determine	Find
Distribute	Give
Effect	Make
Encounter	Meeting
Endeavor	Try

Execute	Carry out
Expedite	Rush
Explicit	Stated
Facilitate	Make easy
Generate	Produce
Implementation	Implement
Lengthy	Long
Maintenance	Upkeep
Materialize	Develop
Modification	Change
Motivation	Drive
Notwithstanding	Despite
Optimum	Best
Origination	Source
Preparatory	Planned
Procure	Obtain, Buy
Proficiency	Skill
Replacements	Replace
Resourcefulness	Resourceful
Standardization	Standardize
Utilize	Use

BETTER WORD: CHOOSE IF IT FITS

Afraid	Terrified
Angry	Furious
Bad	Atrocious
Beautiful	Exquisite
Big	Immense
Bright	Dazzling
Capable	Accomplished
Clean	Spotless
Clever	Brilliant
Cold	Freezing
Conventional	Conservative
Dirty	Squalid
Dry	Parched
Eager	Keen
Fast	Quick
Fierce	Ferocious
Good	Superb
Happy	Jubilant
Hot	Scalding
Hungry	Ravenous
Large	Colossal
Lively	Vivacious

THE CHARTS

Loved	Adored
Neat	Immaculate
Old	Ancient
Poor	Destitute
Pretty	Beautiful
Quiet	Silent
Risky	Perilous
Roomy	Spacious
Rude	Vulgar
Serious	Solemn
Small	Tiny
Strong	Unyielding
Stupid	Idiotic
Tasty	Delicious
Thin	Gaunt
Tired	Exhausted
Ugly	Hideous
Valuable	Precious
Weak	Feeble
Wet	Soaked
Wicked	Villainous
Wise	Sagacious
Worried	Anxious

EXPENDABLE WORDS

We use these words by habit. We can eliminate many.

About	Even
Active	Every
Actively	Exactly
Actual	Fairly
Actually	Feel
A Little	Finally
Almost	Herself
A Lot	Himself
Any	In Fact
Anyway	In General
As	In Order To
At The Present Time	In Particular
Began To	In Spite Of The Fact That
Both	Instantly
By Means Of (By)	In The Event That (If)
Careful	In The Future
Certainly	In The Past
Considering The Fact That	Is/Was/Were
Definitely	Just

THE CHARTS

Kind Of	Proceeded To
Like	Quite
Meaningful	Rather
Merely	Real
Namely	Really
Nearly	Relatively
Necessarily	Seem
Needless To Say	Slightly
Next	So
Now	Some
Of Course	Somewhat
Overall	Sort Of
Overtime	Sort Of
Owing To The Fact	Specific
Particularly	Started To
Perhaps	Such
Per Se	Suddenly
Pretty	That
Probably	Themselves

CONTINUED ▽

EXPENDABLE WORDS (CONT'D)

Then	Used To
Think	Usually
Total	Very
Unfortunately	Which

FACIAL EXPRESSIONS

Absent	Expressionless	Taut
Appealing	Pleadingly	Thoughtful
Beatific	Quizzical	Tight-Lipped
Black	Radiant	Unblinking
Bleak	Roguish	Unreadable
Brooding	Sardonic	Vacant
Bug-Eyed	Scowling	Wan
Curious	Set	Wanly
Dark	Shamefaced	Wide-Eyed
Darkly	Slack-Jawed	Withering
Deadpan	Sly	Wolfish
Doleful	Smiley	Worried
Downcast	Straight-Faced	Wry
Dreamy	Straight Face	
Etched	Sullen	

POWERFUL VERBS

Absorb	Bust	Deposit	Expand
Advance	Capture	Detect	Explode
Advise	Catch	Deviate	Explore
Alter	Chap	Devour	Expose
Amend	Charge	Direct	Extend
Amplify	Chip	Discern	Extract
Attack	Clasp	Discover	Eyeball
Balloon	Climb	Dismantle	Fight
Bash	Clutch	Download	Fish
Batter	Collide	Drag	Fling
Beam	Command	Drain	Fly
Beef	Commune	Drip	Frown
Blab	Cower	Drop	Fuse
Blast	Crackle	Eavesdrop	Garble
Bolt	Crash	Engage	Gaze
Boost	Crave	Engulf	Glare
Brief	Crush	Enlarge	Gleam
Broadcast	Dangle	Ensnare	Glisten
Brood	Dash	Envelop	Glitter
Burst	Demolish	Erase	Gobble
Bus	Depart	Escort	Govern

Grasp	Jostle	Oppress	Probe
Gravitate	Journey	Order	Prune
Grip	Lash	Paint	Realize
Groan	Launch	Park	Recite
Grope	Lead	Peck	Recoil
Growl	Leap	Peek	Refashion
Guide	Locate	Peer	Refine
Gush	Lurch	Perceive	Remove
Hack	Lurk	Picture	Report
Hail	Magnify	Pilot	Retreat
Heighten	Mimic	Pinpoint	Reveal
Hobble	Mint	Place	Reverberate
Hover	Moan	Plant	Revitalize
Hurry	Modify	Plop	Revolutionize
Ignite	Multiply	Pluck	Revolve
Illuminate	Muse	Plunge	Rip
Impart	Mushroom	Poison	Rise
Inspect	Mystify	Pop	Ruin
Instruct	Notice	Position	Rush
Intensify	Notify	Power	Rust
Intertwine	Obtain	Prickle	Saunter

CONTINUED

POWERFUL VERBS (CONT'D)

Scamper	Slump	Stroll	Uncover
Scan	Slurp	Struggle	Unearth
Scorch	Smash	Stumble	Untangle
Scrape	Smite	Supercharge	Unveil
Scratch	Snag	Supersize	Usher
Scrawl	Snarl	Surge	Veil
Seize	Sneak	Survey	Wail
Serve	Snowball	Swell	Weave
Shatter	Soar	Swipe	Wind
Shepherd	Spam	Swoon	Withdraw
Shimmer	Sparkle	Tail	Wreck
Shine	Sport	Tattle	Wrench
Shock	Sprinkle	Toddle	Wrest
Shrivel	Stare	Transfigure	Wrestle
Sizzle	Starve	Transform	Wring
Skip	Steal	Travel	Yank
Skulk	Steer	Treat	Zap
Slash	Storm	Trim	Zing
Slide	Strain	Trip	
Slink	Stretch	Trudge	
Slip	Strip	Tussle	

SECTION III

USEFUL ADVICE

PAUSES

Do's and Do Not's

The pause is your friend, use him…don't abuse him.

Alan Alda says, "It is the space between the lines that makes it a great performance."

Musicians say, "The music is between the notes, not in the notes."

It's not how you construct a pause, it's what is the pause's objective.

We convey messages not only by words, but by pauses. A pause gives your reader or your audience time to process what's been presented.

"Here the pause says, Take the time to understand or react to what's been presented."

Pause: the gold standard.

Rest	Demurred
Took A Breath	Wait A Moment
Took A Break	Wavered
Hesitated	Falter
Froze	… (Short Pause)
Stopped	—(Long Pause)
Deliberate	

THE MEANINGS OF EYE COLORS

Black: night, secrecy, mysticism, goddess, intuition, sex, and magic.

Blue: wide-open sky, sun energy, electricity, the power of conscious thought.

Brown: Brown is a strong and rich color that has connotations of earth-energy, creativity, simplicity, strength, and fertility.

Gray: Gray is a fluid and subtle color that has connotations of water, weather, changeability, mysticism, and wisdom.

Green: Green is a vibrant and fresh color that has connotations of life-force, vegetation, rejuvenation, youthfulness, and health.

Hazel: Hazel is an exciting combination of the inner strength and independence of brown.

Violet: Violet is an exquisite and sophisticated color that has connotations of spirituality, nobility, psychic energy, and purity.

USEFUL ADVICE

UNIVERSAL EXPRESSIONS OF EMOTION

The opportunity to show emotion rather than tell about emotion.

Surprise: Jaw drops, opening the mouth without tension; eyes open widely; brows raised; high and curved; forehead wrinkles horizontally throughout.

Fear: Lips tense stretch, stretch and drawn; brows are raised, drawn together; forehead wrinkles horizontally in the center only; back; eyes open with lower lid tense and upper lid raised in the center only.

Disgust: Upper lip raises and nose wrinkles; lower eyelids move upward; brows are lowered.

Happiness: Corner of the lips drawn upward, and nasolabial fold becomes prominent; eyelids raised, and wrinkles appear around the eyes.

Sadness: Lips tremble and corners drawn downward; eyes may tear; inner brows raised.

Anger: Lips tightly closed; eyelids tense; brows are lowered and drawn close together; wrinkling between the brows.

Physiological signs of anger:

Rapid heartbeat	Sweating
Stomach cramps	Redness of the face
Tightening of the body	Body shaking

CONTINUED ▽

UNIVERSAL EXPRESSIONS OF EMOTION (CONT'D)

Hands shaking
Clenched jaw
Teeth grinding
Headache

Ringing in the ears
Feeling of burning or cold through the body

SELECTIVE APHORISMS FOR CREATIVE WRITING

1. "Either write something worth reading or do something worth writing." Ben Franklin

2. "Don't try to figure out what other people want to hear from you; figure out what you have to say. It's the one and only thing you have to offer." Barbara Kingsolver

3. "I try to leave out the parts that people skip." Elmore Leonard

4. "I'm not a very good writer, but I'm an excellent rewriter." James Michener

5. "Write your first draft with your heart. Re-write with your head." From the movie *Finding Forrester*

6. "Creativity is allowing yourself to make mistakes. Art is knowing which ones to keep." Scott Adams

7. "The difference between fiction and reality? Fiction has to make sense." Tom Clancy

8. "A story consists of someone wanting something and having trouble getting it." Douglas Glover

9. "You don't write because you want to say something. You write because you have something to say." F. Scott Fitzgerald

NEUROLINGUISTIC AND OTHER CUES

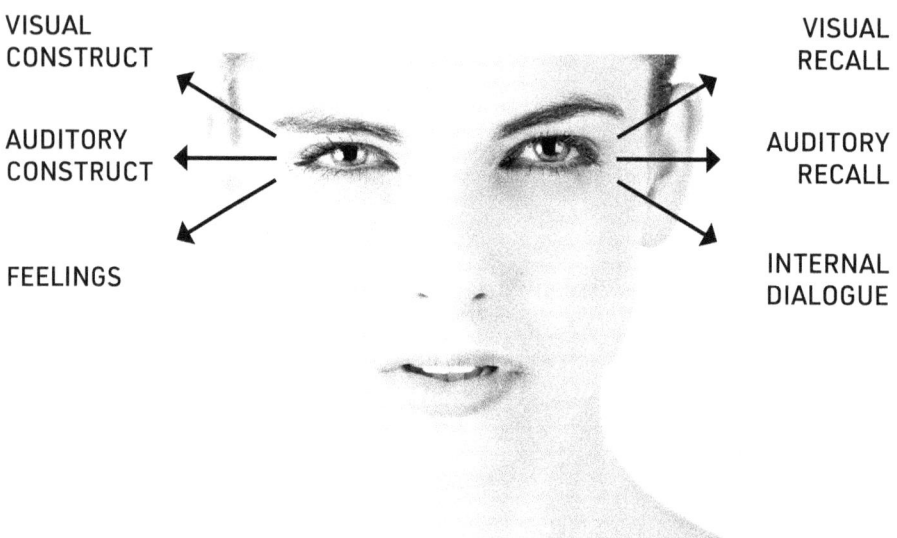

Image by Engin Akyurt from Pixabay

Verbal and nonverbal behaviors can be indicators of truth and deceit. Recognizing these indicators helps writers demonstrate (show) the reader the personality, motivation, and internal conflicts of their fictional characters.

Proponents of Neuro-Linguistic Programming (NLP) claim that certain eye-movements are reliable indicators of lying and indicate the parts of the brain they're accessing for recall and construction of memories. For example, a person looking up to their right suggests a lie whereas looking up to their left is indicative of truth telling.

USEFUL ADVICE

Other clues include:

1. Behavioral paused and delays.
2. Verbal/Non-verbal disconnect.
3. Hiding mouth and eyes.
4. Throat clearing and swallowing.
5. Hand to face activities.
6. Grooming gestures.
7. Shoulder shrugging.

These tools may be useful, but don't use them ham-handedly…subtlety rules.

COMMON CREATIVE WRITING MISTAKES

1. Poor handling of dialogue: realistic, but not too realistic.
2. Unusual characters: reader won't care about them.
3. Unlikable characters: reader won't relate to characters they dislike.
4. Predictability: surprise the reader.
5. Use of clichés: your characters can use them, you can't.
6. Lack of pacing: vary pacing.
7. No sense of setting: sense of place and time.
8. Lack of conflict: no conflict—>no reader interest.
9. Writing: go with the flow. Edit later.
10. Using the popular genres of the moment rarely works.

ABOUT THE AUTHOR

Born in Brooklyn, New York, Lawrence (Larry) W. Gold attended medical school in Chicago. Larry served as a Battalion Surgeon in Vietnam, where he ran the emergency room in an evacuation hospital outside Saigon. He worked twenty-three years in a hospital-based practice in Berkeley, California, and served as Chief of Internal Medicine and Family Practice.

He brings his medical background to his fiction writing, which includes over twenty medical thriller novels. *The Write Word at the Right Time* was borne of a thick, three-ring binder that sat for years at his side.

Larry makes his home in California where he's working on his next novel (and still using the word "said" a little too often.)

OTHER WORKS BY LAWRENCE W. GOLD

Fiction Brier Hospital Series:

First, Do No Harm	State of Mind
No Cure for Murder	The Doctors' Lounge
The Sixth Sense	Out of Darkness
Tortured Memory	Vector Red
The Plague Within	Stranger in a Strange World
Trapped	Justified
Hybrid	Just in Time
Never Too Late	Retribution

Other Novels:

For the Love of God	Deadly Passage
Rage	A Simple Cure

Non-Fiction:

Talking To Your Doctor, a lighthearted look at the doctor/patient relationship

All available in print, Kindle, and most as audiobooks.

www.ingramcontent.com/pod-product-compliance
Lightning Source LLC
Chambersburg PA
CBHW070759050426
42452CB00012B/2408